MOORINGS

Caitlin Press Inc.
3375 Ponderosa Way
Qualicum Beach, BC V9K 2J8

www.caitlinpress.com

Text and cover design by Vici Johnstone
Cover photo: Focussed Images

Printed in Canada

Caitlin Press Inc. acknowledges financial support from the Government of Canada and the Canada Council for the Arts, and the Province of British Columbia through the British Columbia Arts Council and the Book Publisher's Tax Credit.

Library and Archives Canada Cataloguing in Publication
Moorings / Christopher Levenson.
Levenson, Christopher, 1934- author.
Poems.
Canadiana 20230204007 | ISBN 9781773861272 (softcover)
LCC PS8573.E945 M66 2023 | DDC C811/.54-dc23

MOORINGS

poetry

CHRISTOPHER LEVENSON

CAITLIN PRESS 2023

*As always, for Oonagh
and in memory of Kieran Egan*

CONTENTS

Lost and Found: A Sequence

1

A single sock, bus tickets, a quarter
swaddled in lint in a back pocket,
a rosary of phone calls that peters out
in sorry apologies, treks to a dusty office
in airport or concert hall—forget the trivia
and troves of things not so easily
replaced—prescription glasses, watches,
credit cards, even a wedding ring.
There's no end to what is lost. Focus instead
on a best friend struck down in his prime,
a lost chance of making good on a promise,
a love that did not work out.
Above all, know when to give up.

2

Mudlarks scour the City's riverbanks, hoping to find
discarded coins, Roman amphorae, pottery shards
as if to establish continuity. Once hit-and-miss,
nowadays radar and metal detectors make
tracking things easier—finders keepers,
not only treasure, also
hidden mass graves, missing persons,
alternate histories.

3

After the loss of life, a jury's findings
or a cenotaph, mass remembrance
or the profit and loss, there's the collateral damage
of sweatshops, factories
that furnish our plenitude

beside dark streams in lands
we never think of and have not visited,
corpses covered up by a balance sheet.

4

Old age makes room for loss, the price of survival.
What anesthesia for best friends dying too soon
and too far away? The scars, the wounds persist.
And sometimes lost friends are found again by chance,
surfacing after fifty years. (But what shall I do
with my love for a whole country that no longer exists?)

5

The chiropractor adjusts my neck and spine
to release built up tensions, the psychiatrist
wants me to let go of suicidal grief.
Likewise, insurance agents calculate loss,
put a dollar value on a child's life.
We settle, come to terms,
try despite failing eyes to see things in perspective.

6

Though I once had
a photographic memory,
those negatives are lost
and will not develop in
the dark room of the future.
With language it's the same:
halfway through a conversation,
I am lost for words, lose the thread, hear
the whole story unravel.
With time, language disintegrates,
not just the words themselves

are lost to dementia, the power
of speech is taken over
by corporate empires, unique
ways of feeling lost
as languages disappear.

7

The same with friends, after a while
with Christmas letters, phone calls unanswered,
I learn to suspect the worst.
But to remove their names
from diaries and calendars
can bring no resolution, no closure.

8

At a loss, briefly we find ourselves
in things noticed in passing.
So many times we are taken
out of ourselves, stumble upon
an organist practicing
at dusk in an empty chapel,
the slant of sunlight thwarted by cloud,
the evening stillness of reeds
at attention by the river's edge;
wind-flickered wild yellow poppies,
peripheral, by the roadside,
in a meadow a single voice
singing but unaware
of any listeners. This is our reward
for what will endure, what is given.

THE PAST IS A FOREIGN COUNTRY

The Map Of Australia

At ten in primary school I was shown
how to mold Alabastine relief maps
of parts of the Empire: I was given Australia,
told to colour mountains brown, the valleys green.
In the centre, a lost interior, all yellow desert,
I sketched in snakes, kangaroos.

Fifty years later
I flew around Australia, crossing the Outback,
but far too high up. I could make out
nothing but emptiness.

Now in a museum gallery I gaze
through stubborn outcrops of rock, yam, eucalyptus
at stories Aboriginal women painted
from sand and red earth, and try to connect the dots
in the threads and fibres from which they wove their dreamings
into galaxies. Slowly these textures fold into
my knowledge of others, myself.

Ordnance Survey

Obsolete now except as collectibles, thanks to
Google Earth's 24-7 intrusion
into our streets and gardens.
Nothing is strange anymore; we are all Peeping Toms
in the furthest corners of New Zealand or Equador.
Though these maps in my childhood, one inch to the mile,
seemed to reveal everything—
chapels, streams, level crossings, footpaths, churches with spires—
they still left us space to explore on foot, to feel our own way.

On kitchen tables before setting out, I imagined contours,
saw a cliff face rear up, pictured the farm by the marsh.
And they were durable: tucked into our rucksacks
along with a picnic lunch and a compass, even when folded
they did not fray. They gave us connection,
security and scale. It was a tangible world.

Insects

An avid gardener, my father was firm on some things, like
"Centipedes good, millipedes bad." I took his word for it
and became a righteous god for woodlouse and cockroach.
Now when I read
of half a million insect species at risk of extinction
in the coming decades because of climate change,
pesticides, destruction of habitat,
I can't play favourites anymore—snow leopards, polar bears—
or bemoan the dearth of monarch butterflies
while scorning hyenas and hagfish.
There are no bad animals, so reluctantly I am
learning to suffer even the most obnoxious
of insects, mosquitoes, hornets, a plethora
of tiny creatures, almost invisible
or like maggots, scrolling cadavers,
ugly crawlers I would once happily
have squashed underfoot, I finally see their place
in the whole great scheme of things,
how it connects, how they all have work to do
in wetlands, wilderness, desert
as prey or predator, sustaining a commonwealth.

Marmalade

A childhood ritual. Handling the cut fruit,
extracting pips, slicing boiled peel in thick wedges,
my mother, alchemist, hovers
over a seething cauldron to transform
magma of Seville oranges, brown sugar, pith
into a chloroform sweetness
that mists the kitchen windows.

An hour or so later she conjures the residue
into a tempered bitterness, drains off the ooze
in clamped mason jars while I with a wooden spoon
cannot wait, dredge heavy steel saucepans
for vestiges of fruit.

Mr. Schlesinger

A Jewish refugee, he probably came
just before the war to our North London suburb
and stayed a while in our house till the authorities
took him away to an internment camp,
maybe the Isle of Man, as an 'enemy alien'
alongside captured Nazis. We never heard of him
again. All that remained were his books,
stowed in a cupboard in my brother's bedroom
'for the duration':
a Muret-Sanders Dictionary, three heavy tomes
of Bismarck's *Gedanken und Erinnerungen*,
Struwwelpeter, and other evidence of scholarship.
Now, with both my parents dead,
he is untraceable. No one is left to ask.
Had he stayed at home in Germany, there would have been
meticulous documents, closure.

Ghost Train

From the years just after the war I remember them
in fairgrounds of battered south coast resorts
or at the far end of piers, their clunky darkness
competing with Wurlitzers and the slot machines
that told your penny fortune or let you almost glimpse
what the butler saw. Outdated Gothic bric-à-brac—
skeletons, witches, blood—and tendrils of flesh
oozing from canvas walls, a makeshift horror
for us too young to have known the real thing.
Those who have never set foot in the past would not understand
how the eight-track massacre's caught in perpetual motion,
how the fairground music and screams will never stop,
how the ghost trains still run on time.

The Wireless

Long before transistors or ghetto blasters,
it squatted Buddha-like on a low brown table,
our household god, not just for wartime's
sonorous hourly bulletins, but afterwards, too.
My mum and dad listened religiously
to *The Brains Trust, Mrs. Dale's Diary,*
and *Dick Barton: Special Agent,* and left to me
the Children's Hour with *Toytown* and Ludwig Koch,
an expert on birds who spoke with a German accent
you could cut with a knife.

Sunday evenings were the worst when they tuned in
to *Grand Hotel,* with Richard Tauber singing
"We are in love with you, my heart and I,"
then Anne Ziegler and Webster Booth and endless waltzes.
In our suburban semi-detached it was
a cut-price dream of Viennese elegance
which I with subteen impatience scorned, unaware,
with my brother newly dead, how little else they lived for.

Apprentice

My mother's parents died in quick succession
when I was only six. I hardly knew them
enough to sense my loss. We were away,
evacuated. Then, at the end of the war
my father's stepmother, grand-mère, emerged from Clapton
every Christmas and Easter to our tidy suburb.
Afraid of the Tube, she took buses across town,
her brown leather shopping bag creaking with goodies.
With a perennial cold, she reeked of eucalyptus.
Since she was stone-deaf, we had to shout in French:
"*Nous allons maintenant au Jardin des plantes!*"
What *did* the neighbours think?
     When my turn came around, and with no role models
I slowly learnt on the job, driving Aaron to early morning
hockey or baseball practice, telling him bedtime stories,
for the most part just an apprentice, being there. So, undetected
a pinch of an herb or spice will make up the dish's flavour.

Upwords

> *Success is counted sweetest*
> *By those who ne'er succeed*
> —Emily Dickinson

It is our after-dinner ritual.
Every day I am beaten by Oonagh at Upwords,
a three-dimensional Scrabble.
Though I am a forty-year veteran
of teaching high school and college English,
it doesn't matter.

So while I'm wondering if I'll ever find
an opening in our game for newly found words
like 'soffit' or 'lovage'
and despair that 'onyx' or 'zygot' will ever fit,
she lays down letters in an unpredictable sequence,
says, "Well, it *looks* like a word."
And sometimes, dammit, she's right
and I lose again.

This routine humbling is a small price to pay
for all that exists between us and beyond words.

The Ward
(St. Wulstan's TB Hospital, Malvern, 1953)

Converted from wartime use, the barrack wards
breed silence, build a prison of rest.
Winter outside, inside a starchy whiteness
patrolled by nurses. Bill lay there, reading, listless,
long scars across his back where first a third
of one lung had been excised then two thirds of the other,
with at night only a radio's muted hum to staunch the darkness.
Next to a snapshot of his wife, he'd scrawled
a line from Seneca: "The first step to the cure
is desiring to be cured." The pumps still drained him,
the blood tolled in his chest. He did not make it.
One morning his bed was empty. No farewells
from his mates. Only the changed white sheets.

LATECOMER

Latecomer

A latecomer to Canadian history, in '68
I stood at the edge of the party, looking on,
innocent, yet complicit, coming into
a land already 'settled,' its soil broken
by homesteaders, Chinese labourers, Black
railway porters.

Coming from the UK, I did not see,
and had not been schooled to ignore,
First Nations people abandoned in villages
with no clean water, mould on the walls,
hunting and trapping made impossible,
their native tongues forbidden.

I see now how I am tarnished
by a heritage I did not share
and have to learn by osmosis
what others were born to—
the Christie Pits, the Winnipeg General Strike,
the Indian Acts, Africville.
That past is no longer exotic.

Like a many coloured coat
I take upon myself the host
of past injustices and see myself become
part of the landscape...

Aubades

Where all night long brisk cubes
of office and board rooms
asserted their vacancy,
now with tentative fingers
light gropes through crevices,
secreting openness.
Morning has surfaced.

Condos like theatre flats
stacked against low horizons
are hauled out of storage.
The day stages a comeback.

As if over water meadows
the half light infiltrates.
Slowly colour suffuses
the face of the earth.

Light corners the market hall
by Burrard Inlet, picks out
the pennants on marquees.
The day is primed.

Soundlessly from here,
threading the seamless dark
wing lights of distant planes
with flashes of silver slope down
for their final landing approach.

Beyond Our Windows

Beyond our windows I see
the apartment surrounded by
solicitudes of green.
Though only the brightest sun
can infiltrate this shade,
when faint breezes intervene
to shuffle intricacies
of foliage and bough,
by a sleight of leaf it seems
drifts of fritillaries
settle upon my palm
and I feel my pulse tricked into
precarious happiness.

The Fridge

Its white bulk a microcosm
and midden for future archeologists:
beyond the bare necessities, bread and milk,
a jar of artichoke hearts and slices
of smoked beef tongue, honeydew melons.

With no mantlepiece or china cabinet,
it serves as a show-and-tell for occasional guests.
Its impassive front, beset with magnets,
is decorated like a five-star general,
to hold us in place, deep-freeze our memories.

Along with a list of daily medications
and emergency phone numbers are juxtaposed
ironic holiday postcards from old friends,
snapshots of our blended families—
Helen, aged five, riding a tricycle;
and my grandkids in Montreal.

And button relics of a more mobile past,
an unholy trinity—Che Guevara, Castro, Allende—
activism congealed in permafrost.

At The Optometrist's

Hurrying in from the rain,
I register, take a seat.
Then, forehead and chin held steady,
first the left eye then the right
is ambushed by sudden flashes,
bright lights, multi-coloured strobes
probing my retina.

I am under a spell.
As the drops in each eye
take effect my vision blurs
till, wide-eyed as any toddler,
this would-be man of letters
is back in kindergarten,
reciting a random alphabet.
Or is this another language
I have had no time to learn?
To survive must I become
fluent in gibberish?

When I at last emerge
the same wet street half blinds me;
my measure has been taken.

Music in the Morning

Once a month every winter elderly ladies
and a few scattered elderly gentlemen
besiege the Conservatory with their canes and walkers
intent to audit the best quartets and trios
the place has to offer. After volunteers
ply them with coffee and pastries they take their seats,
tune up for their culture fix. Sedately prepared
to be amused, expectant faces receive
instead the solace of feelings that run too deep
under the ground of their being and are unknowable
except in music. For a little over an hour
age calls a truce. Like amphora their lives still hold
unspoilt, unspilt, a past they had thought relinquished
as they submerge into Haydn, Mozart, Brahms
and are re-collected from piano lessons,
school choirs and orchestras, decades of song
when they were most alive, stills of a time
untolled in the aftermath. Beyond all applause
they cherish gratitude, finding that child again,
however briefly, as they are released
into brusque November's fugue of falling leaf.

At the Races
(Hastings Park, Vancouver)

Not for the horses, excitement, a silver cup,
but to be seen there, millennials arrive in stretch limos
decked out in a flurry of costumes, top hats, fascinators
in every conceivable colour. Miniature gardens
adorn long hairdos bloated with flowers or birds. Anything goes
in this endless cavalcade of chatter and selfies to share
later a thousandfold. They jostle marquees selling beer
in plastic beakers or line up to place their flutters
along with the seedy riff-raff in loud check shirts.
Then tipsy, starry-eyed, they hobble or slouch to join
the crescendo of shouts as a turmoil of horses streaks past
the finishing line and the noise recedes and slowly the payout
                                                        begins.

Now it is all over. Somehow the horses
survive it all, sweat and beauty proudly intact,
and behind them always the mountains.

In Kensington Market

Sitting outside a Tibetan cafe at the end of summer,
I watch women saunter past in saris, salwar kameez,
Jamaican men in dreadlocks and woollen caps jostle
                              through crowds
to conjure a carnival air wherever they go.

Emigrants, refugees, however they got here, shake
kaleidoscopes of race, shuffle the polyglot pack,
stir up a savoury stew of lingos, lifestyles, backgrounds,
tarot cards, reiki, oracles, yoga galore. It takes

all sorts of spiritual make-believe to make a new world
where past and future collide and jar or resolve.
In headscarves and hoodies, tribals from Thornhill or Malton
merge, coalesce, in maelstroms of movement and laughter,

swarm into corner stores, rundown half-derelict shacks,
market stalls, sampling from vegan, halal, kosher, gluten-free
beef patties, ramen, jerky, goat—all you can eat
to the sound of heavy metal, steel bands, bongo drums.

A happy cacophony surges and lulls like the sea.
With everything cool, hot, in style, an oven-fresh fusion
where tattoos meld into graffitied fences, this is what Canada means.
And for now, for this Saturday afternoon, we flaunt
                              our peaceable kingdom.

Touch

Until denied, we do not know our need,
how we crave the comfort of touch, the hands
that reach out to embrace, to make connection,
to have and to hold.

In an art gallery I recognize
untouchable objects of beauty and desire,
accept the rules, do not attempt to stroke
Rodin's *The Kiss* or stow away inside
Henry Moore's reclining nudes.

A tactile being, at any other time
I'd welcome such dangerous closeness,
a kind of intuitive tact at my fingertips,
easing the way into relationship.

But when the body's out of bounds,
forced to elude my grasp,
I am in solitary.
Virtual is never enough:
soundbites on Facebook or Twitter
remain unrequited, cannot replace
even the most innocent
pressure on shoulder or hand.

Iona Beach Park, April 2020

Beyond the industrial park
a sullen overcast sky
is dredged of all light.

Why drive out here, unless
for sustenance, or at least
some interim content?

Though distanced, too far away,
at the end of a miles-long jetty
and beyond earshot

the grey of the Salish Sea
at low tide, the blurred horizon,
answers my mood. Oonagh and I,

becoming beachcombers, stoop
to inspect fragments, tidewrack
of broken clam, crab, mussel

that the gulls discarded. Last night
my watch stopped. Now
with a new battery installed,

I know I can't live outside
time's fragile certainty. As shadows
regroup among the few dishevelled

trees edging the salt flats,
the nearby airport's roar
of arrival, departure, is mute,

the wind barely a whisper. Endless
silence. For now, from here, the sea
is in abeyance. It will return.

Delta

Under a bleached sky
land, water, dispute
their outer limits.
The world is adrift.

Willows and osiers
line the more settled shores.
Who'd guess how overnight,
defying cartographers,
islands, peninsulas, channels
could redefine themselves,
loosen earth's bonds?

Unsettled and silent save
for a few seabirds
and the occasional heron,
the soil disintegrates while silt
entwined with weeds creates
new fragile deposits

and we only look on
as probing tides push into
marshlands, undermine jetties.
At sunset, no longer deceived
by windless distant horizons
awash with promises,
this far inland we're aware
how small our influence is
on the movement of waters.

Cell

As movers reduce our living room
to bare necessities, walls stripped
of prints and paintings,
I watch canyons building up
around us. Encircled by cartons—
Cedar Creek, Absolut Vodka,
Pimm's Number One, London Gin—
a lifetime's supply of bottled euphoria
but destined for other gullets,
I gaze around soberly
at all the cardboard orgies,
the late-night party's abandon,
tearful drunken farewells,
and see myself become
reluctant anchorite.

Close to Midnight

Close to midnight
with its diesel idling,
the last bus for downtown
waits, brightly lit, empty.

In the dormant subdivision,
curtains drawn, lawn sprinklers still
at work, garage in lockdown,
kitchen tables set for breakfast,

teenagers in basement rooms
reach out round half the globe,
interconnect, speak freely,
seemingly more at home
in distant continents
though their words
never leave room for silence.

The night accommodates
all kinds, does not ask questions.

BRUSHSTROKES

The Dutch Golden Age Exhibition

The gallery is a cool place to escape
the summer's heat, the heat of the century,
and so well organized:
Merely follow the arrows, listen to headphones,
put your mind in reverse four hundred years.
Admire the crisp detail of a battle at sea,
the flag's snap in the wind, a sailor drowning.
Or examine the still-life set piece where flowers overflow
in intricate decay, *memento mori*
and the burgher's wife in an immaculate ruff
who counters your glance with a righteous steady gaze.
Then focus on alehouse scenes with drunken brawlers
and kitchens awash with children and pets, the play of light
encroaching on darkened boudoirs, the pride of possession.
Finally take in side exhibits that show
how oil paints were mixed, canvases carefully primed.
These artists left nothing to chance.
                Nor does the gallery:
Climate-controlled and lovingly curated,
expertly cleaned, the blinds and screens adjusted
to diminish the world outside. From this safe distance
in our well-lit holding cell we strive to deduce
behind varnished particulars their everyday,
the stench, the heat no one could get away from.

Boudin

The tremulous
grey-blue dalliance
of light with water
extends the sandy skyline
into infinity, to blend
with the pale English Channel.
Ladies with parasols raised
against a hesitant sun
seem unaware how silently
evening approaches.

In the Burne-Jones Galleries

In the Burne-Jones galleries girls' wayward eyes
beseech each passerby from canvas: floribund
philanderers, whose robes and tresses rise
in sinuous profusion, they are summoned
like snakes or hellish flames. Though their flesh prepares
its malign sophistries, languid thighs are enshrined
vainly for the painter, no frond stirs
the ennui of that pale tapestry of mind.

Such sad Victorian splendours! Their desires
no longer fuming vats, attenuate. Lost
in eternal dalliance is the fluted landscape.
Those fugitive virgins rendered unawares
as flagrant as dahlias, gorgeous, gold-embossed,
have merged into art their longing to escape.

Cezanne

The bulk thrust downward juts sideways, at all angles.
Pine woods, rock face, crags
contained in squares, oblongs of colour,
shoulder sturdy cottages aside.
Brusque brush strokes—brown, ochre, olive green—create
from archaic strata, cataracts, dry riverbeds, the sky,
a new underlying vision, restore them to nature
as they compress hillsides, fracture
man's blocked out domain into counterpoint.
Once seen, who can break free?
These shapes herd our way of seeing, concentrate
fissured earth and unrelenting sun, score
into our minds forgotten harmony.

Chardin

You stick to the matter at hand, have a keen eye
for textures, fabrics:
crude earthenware jugs, the kitchen maid's
linen apron, candle holders, a pewter dish.
When you give objects their due, nothing
is mere ornament. You catch
the effect of smoke on the ceiling, observe
how woodgrains on stool and bench
affirm reality, can sense
where hands have lingered, fondled
pine or oak chests of drawers, where peasant feet
have worn away the flagstones.
Straw, copper kettle, cauldron, lead grate, broom
are all in their place. Custodian, you curate
the simple life of parlour and scullery; your brush,
ennobling the ordinary, makes sacrosanct
the silence of steady work, absorbing light.

Daumier

Mists flowing up from the river. Obscurity.
Emerging from a muted world, dark outlines
solidify into a washerwoman, heaving
herself with one small child in tow
up stone steps from the Seine.

So it is: from breeding tenements
the poor, ground down, are trudging to seek redress
in dusty corridors, waiting as shafts of sunlight
pick out gold threads in the Law's gowned eminence.

At the Degas Exhibition

Ballerina, racehorse, jockey:
how your artistry sought to catch
the body's utmost, stretched
almost beyond endurance,
haunches and tendons taut
to withstand, to summon the grace
of overcoming.

And then as counterpoint,
the whole bourgeois
milieu, heavy drapes,
sturdy industrialists
with stovepipe hats at the club,
faces uncreased as their morning coats,
inspecting cotton,
reclining *en famille.*

Under it all, behind
theatre and stock exchange,
women bear down
on ironing boards to urge
a crease out of stiff shirt fronts.
It is their job, they yawn.

In all those canvases,
across the orchestra pit from the wings,
how much the black imposes,
foreshadows their marble torsos,
how the aesthetic sweats
to rein them in,
to control and render pure
the world's agility.

Delvaux

The tram is always just about to depart
from the tree-shadowed terminus at the city's edge.
Strange women of the night, bare breasted, emerge
from archaic palaces. Staring ahead of themselves,
they are deployed like statues along the lamplit vistas.
Through green obscurity the tram bell rings once only.
We are alone. All that remains of the past
is immobilized. Nothing is ever going to move again.

Feininger

Flicker and vortex of sails
the yachts'　flash and intersect
to divide the blue　　horizons, a keen
breeze blowing　the sheets
brace, flap slackly　ropes take the strain,
waves splinter the sun　as immaculate keels
glide through,　movement　solidified.
All is light to your
milling imagination,　flakes of day
fly up　sparks from a grindstone,　chaff
as you invent a scaffolding—
nave, flying buttress, spires—
splicing out of thin air, sea wind
cathedrals of colour　as you practise
silent arpeggios　where slanted downstrokes
tones　meld and diverge　in astringent
counterpoint　thrust and parry,　clash
of surfaces.

Generalić

An extension of hoe or rake, the brush
grew for a purpose, like the yoke of oxen
inseparable from its task.
In this remote corner

of Jugoslavia, all art
was applied, the only
drama was in the bars.
They were all farmers together.

With geese their only sentinels,
these villages were content
to stay out of the way
of tourists and militia.

Croat and Serb sowing, reaping,
got on well enough,
all equally in bond to
obstinate soil and weather.

Your paintings throve on darkness,
pricked out with fires or moonlight,
peasant women, cows, gypsy fiddles:
these were known quantities.

Winters, with nothing to do
outside, you'd take your brush
and in broad strokes sketch
the land's brutal nakedness.

Then darkness returned with a vengeance.
Now there is no peace.
It is winter all the time,
the only harvest corpses.

Goya

You always stood to one side,
observing, not part of the action, making your own way
between regal facades, discredited majesty.
Not seduced by brocades, intricate tapestries
you painted what you saw, the whole spectrum
of human suffering, shawled, huddled peasant women,
the textures of poverty. You watched
as sodden farm hands, knife grinders, stable boys
relished the sugar high of instant freedom. Your brushstrokes caught
their blundering flesh and blood, riddled with bullets
and ignored by official history, your darkening palette
took down all talk of glory, did not turn aside
from Reason's guillotine, showed us war, revolution,
as it really was—Saturn devouring his son, a gnawed-off torso
engraved on our memory. Bringing them down to Earth,
you saw, foresaw. No one else, as you did
could look straight into the brutal darkness, make out
the shapes others refused to see.
Now every time the future horror surprises us,
we should have known. You knew.

Guardi

Mulled silences:
obsidian waters heal
over the drowned man,
a laugh is stifled, gondolas
ply the encroaching dusk.
Suggestions only, shape
of a cloak scarcely descried
through dubious alleyways
or, shadowed by fans, the mask
of a grin or a frown, faces
turned aside, inside out.
It is all show, facades,
this city, these canals, as cobalt
evening makes ready to anchor.

Hopper

If American cities can be beautiful
without prancing equestrian generals
that seal off grandiloquent vistas
or classical gods adorning the balustrades
of Renaissance palaces, you showed us how.
Railway platforms at dawn, a late-night diner
bloom with an eerie light. The rooming house parlour
is haloed by morning sun,
at a filling station on the Merritt Parkway,
all night gas pumps gleam like totem poles.
But beyond all these the salt flats, the dunes, the sea
in the mind's eye persist. Scoured clapboard houses peer
across the strait to islands. You made everyday poetry.

E.J. Hughes

No air could be that still, no cove or mountain range
so miraculously clear. And the paint on houses and barns…!
No matter: for the sake of the tiny jetty
I suspend my disbelief,
and for the ferries breaching the headland, the fir trees, sequoias,
the lacquered white tugboats, clouds, seagulls, the lot.
Pelican-like I gulp down such high gloss landscapes
clearcut of untidiness, anything random.
Transfixed in time, what I merely glimpse,
this precise island dream of a fresh start.

Käthe Kollwitz
(Self Portrait)

A face incised with grief,
you look askance in wary disillusion
that you so often portrayed
in the process of aging.

I revere how your brush and pencil
explored the hidden darkness
of women workers, strikers, all the downtrodden—
the way your art, in charcoal, woodcut, bronze,
enfolds all humanity.
               Across two wars
you held the line, steadily weathered
vast realms of suffering.

Matisse

Primary—waves, olive headland, sky,
azure, vermillion: it took genius simply
to see, to imagine the simple
under its crust of custom, to think
again in surfaces, so that these florid women
could unfurl their limbs into foliage, play among
the pleasantries of light. Your brushstrokes make
flagrant colours lift off
above the palms and bougainvilleas
into the blue of morning.
From flesh tones, the interface
of venetian blinds and sunlight,
you fashion a sanctuary.

Nolde

Standing out in the fields in the spring rain
you let the light pour over you
and break upon the prism of your mind
with blessings that cascade into indigo,
scarlet, magenta, and can transform
sunflower, windmill or dark waterway
wherever your imagination broods.
In this north land
you grew from stone and pasture like a tree
with roots so deep even the Nazis
could never dislodge you from your blood and soil.

Georgia O'Keeffe

Gone now the virulent
inwardness of flowers, their craving
purple and ochre gullets,
your hewn face, furrowed like nature's
baked landscapes of skull, adobe, rock,
is reduced over decades to bone,
slowly erodes, takes on canyons, agave,
crowds in, concentrates
into mesa, red earth.

In the late photographs,
welder of colour, artisan of light,
you have been honed to abstraction,
you have become the mountain.

Composition

For Christopher Pratt

Always the sea outside
presses into the room.
intrudes on stairway and door
yields to an early dawn
the primer has taken,

its luminous calm
Night's stark geometry
then slowly the beach
till by high noon
light is everywhere.

Abstract, it battens down
beyond winter marshes
a stillness breeds,
that spread and infiltrate
of closed houses protected

on breakwater and buoy;
from the basalt shore
gradations of emptiness
venetian blinds
only by shadow.

In this sealed, muted light
from the naked acts of the mind
This balancing eye
Windless and sunless,
these minimal landscapes

nothing distracts
composing, restoring.
can change the world you see.
they pull to eternity,
merging with the sky.

THE CAMPS

Camps

No trace remains. To an act of faith I owe
my patchwork identity: every so often I enter
the mineshaft of memory, burrowing through
discarded diaries and letters to uproot
places and people I knew decades ago,
seemingly desperate to restore
that frayed network of connection,
to "move about in worlds not realized."

It was another country and, except for two school trips,
my first time abroad, a mere eight years
since newsreels had shown us human
stick insects emerging from Buchenwald, Treblinka.
After the Dutch floods of '53
relief teams—Mennonites, Quakers, Brethren—
assembled in Oude-Tonge, Zeeland, alongside
young Germans—Eva, Dietrich, Hans, and Rosemarie.
Like prisoners we spent long days cleaning bricks,
sorting debris from the wrecked homes
of those displaced or drowned.
Evenings we gathered, crouched around campfires,
to share folksongs from our homelands—
"Kein schöner Land, Auf der Lüneburger Heide"—
as a makeshift antidote to all we had undergone.
In smoky melodious rituals we knit
seine nets of brief community through song.

Sixty-five years later, the nuclear waste of my youth,
though buried, is still not depleted. How come I did not know
those words would come home to me, the air
grow thick with whisperings?
When, exiled into ourselves, we all took off

in the prevailing headwinds of history,
some names stayed with me, disinterred
from old address books: a Swiss girl, Lux-Marie;
Einar from Norway; the Italian, Giorgio,
addicted to 'jig-a-jig'; Turkish Elise; Manuel
from Venezuela; two Americans, Marilyn, Jane…
But mostly silence takes over.
I finger their names like worry beads, think how past lives
have been translated into the everyday
and wonder who, where they are, how many have died.

None of us could have foreseen
the aftermath—Berlin Wall, the Cuban crisis,
China's Cultural Revolution—nor resisted the wind tunnels
that dispersed us all like thistledown into a world
that left scant room for songs or brotherhood.
What became of our ambitious will to do good?
I have grown allergic to hope.
Though words in a dozen languages lie round
like bricks from flooded homesteads, ready to be
cleaned and repurposed, we are trapped
in the world wide web. We do not communicate.

Vast swarms of locusts descend,
devouring memory.

I tell myself: "Do not resuscitate."

Another Country

Countries do not disappear like bodies bulldozed
into a mass grave. This was never a desert;
some things always outlast oblivion.
From surviving unshredded records
we learn to transliterate place names, decode
the cries of the dispossessed.
Context and texture cling like scraps of skin
to the long-buried corpse exhumed.

But no matter how skilled, archeologists
cannot dig up the heart, the beating pulse
that made this a homeland. What's handed on,
concealed behind curtains, urn-prisoned,
has no further use for us, living.
What I need to know is
"Where the school was, the well, what songs the children
used to sing as they made their way home."
Where was the mosque, the market,
before these villages vanished?

So much twisted history,
So much we will never know.

Return

In the refugee camp after the Naqba his mother and father
were constantly knitting fishing nets.
When he asked why, he was told
"This way, the day you return to Tiberias,
you'll have everything you need to start afresh."
His parents, now drowned in all but memory,
assured him that the deeds to their house by the shore
and to their boat were still valid, and merely await his return.

Neutrality: A Footnote

(May 1940)

A British official's diary entry for May 4:
"Home at eight. Dined and worked.
Planning conquest of Iceland for next week.
Shall probably be too late!
Saw several broods of ducklings."

When neutral Denmark fell to invading Germans,
Iceland, land of the Viking Sagas, but also the site
of the Althing, the world's first
democratic parliament, might have been next.
Britain reacted haphazardly:
under Colonel Robert Sturges some new recruits,
seven hundred marines, not even equipped
with rifles, and many seasick,
cramped on board the HMS Berwick and HMS Glasgow.
They took firearms training on deck.
With few maps, mostly poor, one drawn from memory,
and no one knowing the language,
they came ashore before dawn at Reykjavík,
met no resistance, arrested the German Consul,
disabled communications, commandeered vehicles,
occupied radio stations, landing areas,
'to secure the North Atlantic' and maintain
the naval blockade of Germany.

Though Iceland's official neutrality lasted till war's end
it was not observed by the occupying troops:
British, Canadians, Yanks found Iceland's women
open to truce, or more. Some came back with them
to the New World; they leave us picturing
alternative histories.

Code

Years it took them at Bletchley during World War Two
to decipher the Nazi code, to elicit meaning
from seemingly random numbers and letters,
but at least they knew what they were looking for
and the cost of failure. Nowadays we are inured
to passwords, computerspeak, and handy with acronyms.

But entering the boardrooms, homes, country clubs
of those you presume are friends, nothing's as simple
as morse or semaphore: a quizzical raised eyebrow
from a regimental blazer and tie, deferential
smiles in the face of authority, this is the minimal
acknowledgement of someone 'not one of us,' an outsider.
A nod and a wink, a shoulder turned away,
a special handshake, pat phrases falling in place,
an accent noted, a wrong address, and you
are filtered out. No one can teach you
this international language, no grammars exist,
you read between the lines.

Shredder

... and arise, arise
From death, you numberless infinities
Of souls, and to your scatter'd bodies go; ...
　　　　　　　　　—John Donne

Valuing my privacy, I consign
bank statements, medical data, cancelled cheques
first to the shredder then the recycling bin.
So too on Judgement Day, however we die—
by plane crash, apartment fire, avalanche, riot police—
will a patient God painstakingly like the East Germans
sift through shredded Stasi files to establish guilt,
expose secrets long withheld, and then be able
to make some sense of each of our billion
reunified fragments?

Drone

On paper it seemed like a good idea—
surgical strikes zeroing in, taking out
known terrorists, a laser targeting
one rogue cell in the body politic.

Unlike the drone of a thousand bomber raid
where, high above compassion, navigators
connected dots of fire in the darkened cities,
this is more accurate.

Even so there are always mistakes
Through faulty intelligence Pakistani villagers,
no matter who their kin, terrified families,
crouch under collapsing walls, collateral.

In the White House and the Pentagon,
robotic bureaucrats with clean hands
and cooler heads prevail and see 'the big picture'
without the distorting lens of imagination.
As with a video game whose outcome
leaves no residue, on paper it works well.

Infrastructure

As backhoes heave clay into daylight,
we are overwhelmed by the stench
of repressed, corrupted earth.
It's why we don't look beyond
surfaces, bright facades, placid storefronts.
Why we did not notice
the leaves' frantic semaphore until,
with our cities disabled
by, tornado, flood, hurricane,
we call on sniffer dogs to seek out
the scent of humans.

Asphalt, tarmac, cement
provide the thinnest of skins
over the void. When abruptly
road surfaces give away,
cars and a truck fall into
a gaping sinkhole. Sure
it can be repaired. It is our confidence
that suffers, all we took
for granted.

Erosion

Experts had warned, of course, decades ago
that the soil here was unstable, would sometime give way,
but no one was listening back then; they were busy assembling
shoreline properties, servicing holiday lots and access roads.

Sure, crackpot ecologists were evangelizing doom
but in the resort's lackadaisical, sun-struck sprawl
no one deciphered the shifting alliances
of sand and grass on the dunes or noticed high tides
eating away at the cliff's edge. War surplus gun emplacements
had held back invasion once. No worries: they'd do it again.

It was all over in a matter of minutes:
the slapdash holiday shacks collapsed in dust,
bandstand and boarded up amusement arcade,
ice cream van, dodgem cars, real estate offices
are at one now with the ocean.

Survivalists

As light by light the great metropolis
falls silent, its subways and downtown streets
devoid of traffic, we gather our perishables
and prepare to head for the sheltering forests of legend.

Will we remember obsolete boy scout skills,
tying knots, lighting fires? Will we be able when needed
to kill and skin the animals we loved
to see at a safe distance? How little of what we are
we can carry with us

apart from cooking utensils, knives, matches, an axe
to cut down trees that once we swore to preserve
for our grandchildren's sake, and perhaps some easily portable
musical instrument, maybe a flute?

Also a digital watch, a family photo album
and Annie Dillard's autobiography
to remind us what childhood was like.
If we're lucky we'll find a dry cave
where we can store kindling and memories.

How much do we need to survive?

Threads

1

Big Brothers left a message on my phone:
"We will come by tomorrow to pick up
clean, reusable cast-offs for our thrift store."
Sometimes I visit there, to burrow through
the sartorial trickle-down, wandering a maze
of trenches to finger old uniforms, war surplus,
along with magazines, the rubble of spent lives,
abandoned finery. What am I looking for?

2

"Nice threads!" The imperial fashion houses
—Habsburg, Bourbon, Castille—
knew all about power dressing, but also depended on
remainders, planned obsolescence.
What yarns we weave around empire!
As the silver and gold of discarded opulence frayed,
all that survived of their costume drama were cockades
and threadbare tapestries whose heroic names unspool
into oblivion. In uprooted family trees,
their crowns destroyed, maggots unstitch the flesh
of disused majesty, a fabricated past.

3

Forensic pathologists do not find it easy
to salvage threadbare life from simple fabrics,
to interrogate cloth from crumpled jackets left
at the scene of atrocities. How can they pick clean
after all the damage done by rodents, mildew, time,
the unfederated bones? How test stains of semen and blood?
Or set aside from their minds the cries of neighbours,
as they reassemble cleansed fibres to restore
identity to the clamouring anonymous dead?
Yet those that survive still need,
more even than bodies, names.

MOORINGS

Harbour

Clarion light
outlines solid blocks—
a rigid geometry
of warehouse, gantry, crane,
stacks of containers—
their primary colours imprinted
on the greens, mauves, and ochres of
a compliant coastal landscape.

An emptiness of
uncluttered horizontals,
rectangles, rail-spurs, broken
only by hawsers, oil drums.
A lacerating wind
strafes waiting cargoes,
tugs at tarpaulins covering
long-distance trucks.

Few people are needed here
to control all movement,
everything's mechanized.
But beyond the breakwater
impervious seas, bleak horizons
deny the illusion of order.

Airport Hotel

Mere hyphen between travelling and home,
it exudes well-managed neutrality.
Freed from the frenetic, listless drive
of the Arrivals Hall, it is an enclave
of obstinate calm where, dazed, anonymous,
passive, we try to sleep. Behind white blinds
there is nothing to see apart from parking lots,
arc lamps and runways. The room is immaculate,
soundproofed, self contained,
in our inter-connected world a holding pen.
Next morning when we come to, post-op,
our senses re-assemble the room, aware
such limbo cannot last, we face more flight, return.

Frames

From our Glasgow hotel window, I can see
rotundas at either end of a tunnel
built in the 1880s under the Clyde,
and just beyond the car park a huge black gantry,
The Hammerhead, all that is left
of a hundred years of labour.
With sixty-two former shipyards gone, only three remain.
Industry's razed grey areas are up for grabs,
tabula rasa for civic architects.
And where expletive furnace steam once forged
the world's boiler plates and ships screws, a frugal sun
stakes out commercial property lines. Robots take on
the heavy lifting, whole wharves and quaysides
levelled and realigned.

The waves of sound that once reverberated
from the Empire's second city, as across oceans
steel girders fangled here swung into place
and fifty stories high
were riveted into skeleton skyscrapers
have fallen silent now and overseas,
in Singapore, India, Brazil, the long derelict
iron corpses of locomotives are junked
or buried in museums. Here, saved from the scrapyard
alongside a tall ship in Zaha Hadid's
curvaceous new space, they have become antiques.

When Ray and Val come over from Ireland to meet us
at the People's Palace we foraged with them through documents
only a few decades old. The curators force us to share
cobbled yards, outside loos, the kitchen range's black grate—
all things we never thought of as history. At one remove we endure

tenements, shop floors, drunkenness, prison cells,
crowds at a public hanging, and the first stirrings
of unions, labour movements, all that focused skill
discarded, gone to earth. Now, as the city's shades
coalesce into evening, trams sleekly glide
through the subterfuge of public space. A lifetime's experience
loses all value. As individual humans
we are slowly becoming redundant. Where is community when
slipways and wharves re-imagined as civic concourse,
verdant pedestrian malls, transform the places
we gathered to remember things we thought nothing of then,
a simple childhood reframed, forged into something new?
Unseen money and power are absolute, frame our need.

In the Kelvingrove Galleries—a massive Victorian pile
set aside in its own discreet parkland—before proceeding
to its legacy of great portraits, local and foreign,
we were lured to explore artisan handiwork, discover
the way we see, how paint is mixed, the fabric
of canvas, the studio, the brilliant intricacy
of visual creation. As visitors we were framed
to be a part of the learning. We are what we have seen.

But outside on the street again, on pedestrian walkways, in pubs.
I sense the amalgam, the stir-fry of people, happy
to speak with strangers, welcome us, show us the way,
spill their life stories. They form the basic ingredients
of continuity, co-existence, immigrants, refugees
from all points of the abandoned world. They came here to live,
to imagine a future, to frame community.
But how much more time do we have
to construct a durable city, a place we can live with?

Moorings

Waiting as churned waters becalm and the ferry men
manoeuvre the boat's great bulk between barnacled pilings
into the dock, making it fast with hawsers,
circling the bollards with rope, I watch iron plates slide down
so we can disembark, tread solid earth again.

It is an intricate business, growing old.
No handbooks or charts exist for this rocky coast.
We make our own ways slowly between headlands
bewildered in mist, aware of how easily
we could founder on hidden hazards, islands, sandbars.

No wonder then in low season how many wilderness
misfits drift to these shores to test
whether they have it in them to convert
once homeopathic doses of solitude
into community and create from dismantled lives
micro-climates of love and tolerance.

While elderly pony-tailed nomads set up stores
for sporting goods, camping equipment,
earth mothers bottle fruit for farmers' markets.
All summer's a festival, then after the Harvest Fair,
with the tourists gone, ramshackle Trading Posts
are abandoned except for the locals, silenced the call
for handcrafted jewelry, the Museum, a former jail
is locked up for the season. The bookstore opens
only four days a week. All that remains
are essential services—naturopaths, massage, yoga.

As in the lengthening dark we putter about
A-frame cottages limpetted to the shore,
the vagrant smiles of friends make us re-enter
a jungle of memories, ashrams, happenings, demos,
an activist past put on hold. But across the water
beyond the picturesque lighthouse the sunset glow
from the distant metropolis blends
all their lives were and all they might have been.

Face

1 Sediment

When after long absence
I run into old friends,
I am distraught to see,
imprisoned in our skins,
what husks we have become.
Who could have foretold
how age would shadow us?

Though hard enough to confront
the faces we have grown into,
it is harder still to accept
the sediment of grief
thrown by so many years.
No matter with what care
we manicure or retouch,
cosmetics cannot gloss over
wars, childbirth, motherhood,
the turmoil of family.
Past loveliness dissolves,
muscles attenuate.
Cross-hatching that early calm,
time will erode, undermine
foundations that seemed so firm.

2 Confluence

When lives flow into each other
they intertwine so swiftly
we can no longer tell
which tributary streams
of anger, anxiety,

hollowed out cheeks and blurred,
once limpid eyes, wore down
the sturdiest confidence
and which, submerged in sand
shaped new topographies,
a composite of our past.

3 Explorers

What might cartographers trace
from the straits we have passed through
on voyages, explorations?
Our lives are laid out flat
like Mercator projections.
But zero in like Google
on rift valleys and clefts, a whole
topography of loss and exultation
and you see how decades
molded us by attrition.
Everything leaves its mark
as each of us becomes
our own Columbus, Magellan.

4 Body Shop

Testing, testing...
Habitues of doctor's waiting rooms,
prompt with a breathless recital of symptoms,
like the old gas guzzlers we once owned, we too
from time to time are hoisted onto a ramp
for manual inspection: sump, batteries, exhaust pipe,
carburettor—all in turn
are prodded, poked, diagnosed.
However little we trust technology, we are its prisoners.

Often fine-tuning's enough. At other times an essential
unit must be replaced—a pacemaker, hip or knee.
Metal supplants worn cartilage or we undergo
skin grafts from buttocks or thigh. Is what emerges
after the anaesthetic still us, an amalgam?
How long can we defer
that final trip to the junkyard? No matter, I feel okay,
good for a few more miles. I'll drive myself
into the ground.

5 Trees

Keen winds have sheared away
summer's extravagance.
Once shade trees have shed, abandoned
their green uniformity,
they can display their true colours,
crimson, orange, gold
to challenge the sunset's
spectacular flare-up
till slowly November affirms
the shapes of winter.
Now trunk, crown and boughs create
what we'd not seen before,
a stark geometry.

6 Sculptors

Though sharp eye and chiselled jaw
muscle and cartilage
will in time crumble,
nor can good bones alone
secure a smooth repose,
unseen fingers model lost wax,
firm hands of spirit form
in inner darkness

what will become of us.
With surfaces sheared away,
the lines at last come clean.
Sorrow and joy converge
in whittled cheek and brow.
With all excesses gone,
each sculpted face becomes
truly articulate.

From What Deep Wells

For Oonagh

Unbidden, from deep wells
they rise, your tears,
I cannot tell but know
they have been long contained
in childhoods I did not share,
and you no more. They shaped
a brother and sister bond
you can hold onto now
only in solitude. They leave
as watermark the indelible
contours of grief, its highest tide
slowly abating.

Oblivious to
rituals of loss, your face
is draped in silence.
No matter how long since
that death was foreseen
the heart will not lie fallow
and for now what other space
but sorrow, memory?
Words that might staunch the darkness
merely wash over you.

Water will always find
its own level, you alone
know the right moment
to let go, embrace his absence.
As he casts off into the night,
we on the quayside remain,

mere bystanders, tiny figures
waving farewell. Like ours,
your eyes will in time
grow accustomed to the dark.

Permanent Press

In memory of Elise Partridge

A pity you could not be here for me to tell you in person
how, surrounded by garish plastic baskets of washing,
your poems enlivened my hour at the laundromat
and made my decisions—heavy duty? regular? delicate?—
easier, almost a pleasure. Along with trousers and shirts
that like their owners come in all ages, sizes, and colours,
your lines cavort in my mind and help me to treasure
behind slapdash appearance wild hints of hidden meaning,
the permanent press of time and circumstance,
how everything neatly folded will soon get crumpled,
how randomly like our garments we grow stained.

A red lamp flashes on, my time is up, I gather
my clothes still damp from the dryer, sort them, work my way back
to my lodgings, pocketing unused quarters for later visits,
knowing once more what I've lost by your absence,
yet how much remains.

Interlude

For Gary Geddes

After the sounds of summer—the day's last ferry
edging into the wharf, somewhere a mower grazing
a still unkempt lawn, the distant hubbub
of trucks on the Island Highway—
after all this, a healing solitude
spreads like a seine net over everything,
envelops your shoreline home. Like Prospero
you have shown me around your island,
post office, two schools, a dairy farm, a pub,
only three hundred residents, everyone knows you.
At dinner we talk of poetry, mutual friends,
your earlier travels, and the pain of Africa
that grips you still. Then you escort me down
to the guest room, a recent addition that still smells
of freshly sawn wood. That night I sleep well.

Next morning I rise early, explore your dock,
watch hummingbirds, purple finches
crowd round the feeder. Down by the water's edge
a heron practices stillness.

Later, fine weather holding, you take me back
to the ferry. As we wait I gaze across
brief stretches of rippled water taut with sails.
We hug goodbye, uneasily aware
that this might be the last time
before we launch into more permanent silence.

In a Green Shade

In memory of Michael Hamburger

This postcard memento of past happiness
still decorates our fridge, reminds us how
we stayed a few days one summer with you and Anne
at Marsh Acres, your sprawling, partly timbered
sixteenth century home in deepest Suffolk,
a hospitable chaos piled with books.

With words not your only care, you guided us through
the kitchen garden into the apple orchard
where, despite twigs underfoot and unkempt grass,
the gnarled boughs twisted this way and that gesticulated
toward a home-grown Eden.

Yourself as a child transplanted,
you became an unsuspected connoisseur,
understood grafting and how much the soil meant
for fruit trees, how some stocks will take root
and others not. What instinct told you how
to keep fruit warm and dry throughout the winter?

To cultivate your garden
you pruned carefully, took cuttings to secure
maximum flavour, noted each tree's history
then at harvest time could rattle off to us
their individual qualities that like old friends you prized
for crispness and succulence.

Composted, your words become
part of the soil we grow in.

Inukshuk

In memory of Richard Rosenberg, past president of BCCLA and of the
Peretz Centre for Secular Judaism

In the winter of 2010 the Kerrisdale
Community Centre planted an inukshuk—
stacked rocks in human form that serve
as permanent signposts across the Arctic
and an Inuit symbol of hope and friendship—intended here
to honour the Olympic flame that was carried past.

Ten years later under a giant magnolia,
a new bench displays a plaque
'in loving memory of our mothers,
Afser Begum and Bilqis Jahan, to celebrate
their remarkable lives.'

Richard would have been happy to see them together,
and watch how fear and suspicion
slowly erode into civility
so that in the end
we are all citizens.

Memorial Service

A place for celebration, time set aside
for ex-colleagues and friends, fragmented families
to filter into one last time, many of us still shaken
by his late death. Yet as each in turn
ascends to the sunlit lectern, attempting to console
with some revealing tale, a favourite joke,
our solo voices trying to harmonize, we mull
the multiplicities, all we did not know,
how he worked hard for the school board, volunteered
at soup kitchens, homeless shelters, in his last years
took up the ukulele.

But closure? His real presence
dissolves in the mouth. Despite flowers, solemn music
the grief we carry within us
will gestate like a cancer.

Nil nisi bonum... Even so, afterwards,
over wine and cheese, ex-wives and lovers
comparing notes, hoover up
all the decisions postponed,
missed opportunities, the way
his first marriage broke up: we conclude
'he was a very private person,'
his mind a catacomb
that few dared venture into.
Nor have we even now
the right combination to unlock
his peculiar charm.

So, slowly out of the mists of memory
a different person emerges.

Casual acquaintances wonder
how could he reconcile … ?
What was all *that* about?
Who was this stranger?
This was our last chance
to get to know him.
We are still left with questions.

The Travel Section

Mostly nowadays I flicker through quickly, noting
the blue glare of Aegean surf, safari trips
across Kenya, treks in Nepal, before I discard
their glossy come-ons in the recycling bin.
My legs give up on me, sheer willpower's no longer enough
to tackle Machu Pichu or reach Vladivostok
on the Trans Siberian Railway.
In my mind, a world traveller at fifteen,
I retrace forays to London's West End embassies,
gathering brochures for Cyprus, Connecticut—
impossible destinations. Though never lured
by five-star beach resorts or luxury cruises,
I am still game for anywhere unknown.
On that final re-positioning
I'll travel light, take my chances. I am on stand-by.

Acknowledgements

Firstly, to Oonagh, for her constant loving attention to my work in progress, as also to the members of the A-Drift Writers Collective, with whom many of these poems were discussed and improved.

Some poems have appeared in the following magazines:

Arc, Arfur, Canadian Literature, Event, The Maynard, The High Window and *Vallum.* "Touch" appeared in the anthology of Pandemic poetry, *The Sky is Falling! The Sky is Falling!* (Planet Earth Poetry, 2021), and "Two Trees" appeared in the anthology, *Worth More Standing* (Caitlin Press, 2022). Two poems, "Face" and "Frames," were included by David Zieroth as a holm in a recent trio from The Alfred Gustav Press series of chapbooks.

About the Author

OONAGH BERRY PHOTO

Christopher Levenson was born in London, England, in 1934. After working in Germany and the Netherlands and studying in the US, he came to Canada in 1968 to teach English and creative writing at Carleton University in Ottawa. He is the author of thirteen books of poetry, most recently *Small Talk* (Silver Bow Publishing, 2022), and three chapbooks. He was the co-founder and first editor of *Arc* magazine. Levenson was the recipient of the inaugural Eric Gregory Award in 1960 and the 1987 Archibald Lampman Award for *Arriving at Night*, and his collection *Night Vision* was shortlisted for the Governor General's award in 2014. Levenson reviews poetry for the *BC Review* and lives in Vancouver, BC.